Run bare foot ?
Read Bea

GW00394081

Richard

Humphrey wandered through the wood,

Further than a bear cub should.

Searching for berries for his tea,
He saw something shiny by a tree.

"What is that? Is it a shoe?
Hold on a minute, there are two!"

Fly, zoom, boost and air.

He slipped them on, "gosh they're comfy!"

Then skipped home, a happy Humphrey.

His bear cub pals were very jealous.
"Where did you find them? Won't you tell us?"

"I found them there, beyond the hill.
They'll help me run, I'm sure they will."

Humphrey wore the shiny shoes,
Until one day he could not move.

He fell while running down a track.
"Ouch!" He cried, I've hurt my back."

He tried a hop and a skip.
"Ouch!" He cried, "I've hurt my hip."

He tripped and crashed into a tree,
"Ouch!" He cried, I've hurt my knee."

Taking off a shoe he saw
A bright red, painful, shoe-shaped paw!

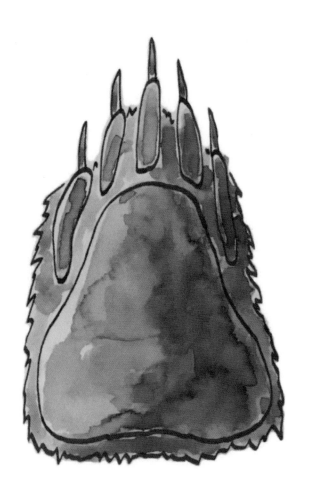

"Without these shoes, my paws were stronger.
I will not wear them any longer."

The other bears were all confused.
"Why leave the shiny shoes unused?"

"They weren't so great, I was misled.
I couldn't feel the ground" he said.

Humphrey spread his claws and smiled.
Without the shoes, he could re-wild.

Bounding barefoot through the trees.
Back to his best, he was so pleased.

"GRROOOAHHH" he roared, on all fours,

Feeling the dirt between his claws.

WHOOSH! He sped through the sand,

Knowing where his paws should land.

CRUNCH!
He trod on
twigs and sticks.

Without the shoes, his paws were fixed.

Author & Illustrator Bio: Richard Jansen

Richard is an endurance runner and student physiotherapist from Somerset in the UK. Inspired by books including Christopher McDougall's 'Born to Run' and Helen Hall's 'Even With Your Shoes on', Richard trains and competes wearing minimalist and barefoot-style shoes. Combining his passions of running and story-telling, Richard creates children's books that encourage natural movement.

Follow @bear.foot.balance on social media and visit bearfootbalance.com to discover more.

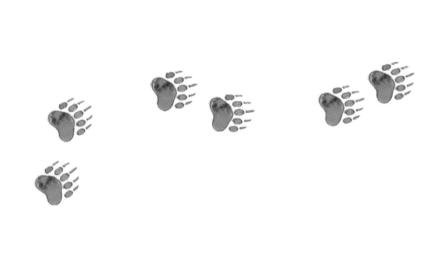